Praise for

"In poems bursting with vulnerability, honesty, and a hopefulness tempered by the hazards of love, Joseph Ranseth, as a fellow searcher, guides us through every dark chamber of the heart and beyond into the light, what some call the soul. Let's Stay Here is an invitation—to pause, poised on each poem where every line is the breath of a friend. You will know this friend well by the time you reach the final stanza. Take the invitation—and stay. These poems will surely stay with you long after you finish them."

Benjamin Cutler, author of *The Geese Who Might be Gods* and *Wild Silence*

"This beautifully written, heartfelt collection of poems brings us back to what matters most in life. To live, to love, and to be our full selves. 'Let's Stay Here' and soak in the warm energy of Joseph's words."

Dr. Ganz Ferrance, Registered Psychologist, Optimal Performance State Expert, Author of *The Me Factor: Your Systematic Guide to Getting What The Hell You Want*

"'*Let's stay here*' is a beautifully crafted collection of poetry that invites readers to explore the depths of love, presence, and self-discovery. Each poem is thoughtfully composed and speaks to the heart, creating a meaningful connection with readers.

"Joseph's poetry is moving, and his ability to capture the essence of life's most profound emotions is remarkable.

"'*Let's Stay Here*' is a poetic journey that I warmly recommend to anyone seeking to embrace the beauty of the present moment and the transformative power of love."

Graham Wardle, Actor, Writer, Podcaster

"Reading through these poems was an exercise in self-reflection. Joseph's journey brings us through the highs and lows of intimate relationships and, ultimately, lands readers in the realm of healing and awareness. A must-read for those who need to be reminded of the possibilities and to reconnect with themselves."

Jalyn C. Wade, Author, *The White Witch's Daughter Trilogy*

"*Let's Stay Here* is a beautiful tale of a man on a journey to understanding love. Joseph's words are raw and intimate. Many of his reflections resonated deeply within me as I reflected on my own relationships. The truths of love that he shares are what I wish every person could come to know. It is a powerful guide to what true love is and where it is found."

Kimberly Clyde, Illuminate Literary Arts

"To say that this collection of poems is excellent is an understatement! Absolutely brilliant! The book tugs at the heart strings, turns the soul inside out to reveal the poignant aspects of relationships, the growing pains of a soul journey. Reading Joseph's poems is both triggering and cathartic. They stand as landmarks for countless others that are also navigating the turbulent rapids of personal growth and healing. The poems pull the reader out of the lightless room of an individual experience into a place of resonance, of relating and being related to. Of recognizing traits of their journey in that of the protagonist. Of being not alone. They empower, give hope, like a pair of wings given to a phoenix that was sure it would never fly again."

Olya Lambert, Author of *Coming To A Place of Oneness*

Early Reader Reviews
for *Let's Stay Here*

"The first time I read this book, I cried.
The second time I read it, I cried.
I hope everyone has the opportunity to be so touched by these words. 10 stars from me!"

"There was not a time where I picked up the book to read it that I wasn't in tears because from the author's pain and vulnerability of his heart, or in tears because I was experiencing beauty in a tiny fraction of the way that he views love and the world around him."

"These words have an innate ability to open your heart and make you reflect on where you are in relation to where you have been. They are soul grounding, and inspired by God."

"*Let's Stay Here* authentically capture the emotion, depth, and beauty of how it feels to fall in love, to fall out of love, and then, to fall in love with one's self again after heartbreak."

"Beautifully written, very emotional."

"I started with compiling a list of the poems that really hit me in the heart strings, and within a few poems I quickly realized I'd be listing nearly every poem in this book. My eyes were constantly glossy, yet I'm not sure if it was from sadness or happiness. Probably a bit of both."

"This book serves as a great reminder as to what love is to anyone who may be stumbling along the way, and a reminder to never ever give up along that journey!"

"I adore this book! These poems are written with incredible openness and deliver a message of profound truth, unlike anything I've ever read before. They speak to my heart in a way that I wasn't expecting, but welcome."

"These words are captivating because they are powerful but also so tender at the same time. I felt like I was getting a glimpse into a remarkable, passionate, and enthralling love story that spoke to my heart and soul, as the story kept unfolding and growing, I was along for an epic ride."

"*Let's Stay Here* belongs in your hands, for your eyes to take in so that its message can be absorbed into your heart."

"This book healed my broken heart."

"I could not hold back the tears… it touched me deeper than I knew was possible."

"Let's Stay Here" by Joseph Ranseth is many wonderful and beautiful things: it is a poetry book, a love story, and a modern-day hero's journey. But perhaps most notably, it is an invitation to heal; to find wisdom in the midst of heartbreak, to uncover hope when hurting, and to recognize ourselves as we traverse the paths of our own lives — upon which we all stand as heroes in our own journeys."

"The message of this book is one of progression. The progression that can come through the heart-wrenching journey of love we all experience, in an often co-dependent world, by learning to find the true power which can only come from within."

"A modern-day Rumi."

"Very beautiful. There is a lot of love and passion in these poems. I read about pain, but I ended up reading about evolution. These poems show us how to be made free."

"To say that this book is excellent is not just an understatement, it's cheap… like putting a price tag on a wedding ring you have worn for a lifetime. There is so much heart and truth in this book. I'm grateful to have found it."

"I was crying from the very first page."

"After finishing the last page, I found myself craving more"

Let's Stay Here

Published by Joseph Ranseth Inc.
56 Goodfellow Way
Winnipeg, MB R3W 0K2 Canada

lovetruthpoetry.com

Cover by Joseph Ranseth
ISBN: 978-0-9813730-4-1 (print)

Printed in USA

Advance Reader Copy

Let's
Stay
Here

Dear future wife,

It was always you.

Table of Contents

Let's Stay Here

Introduction

When I first started preparing this book for publishing, but long before I knew how the story would end, I penned these words as an introduction:

So this book is going to be a love story. At least, I think it will…

I don't know all the details of how it will unfold, but I do know how it will end: exactly as it should.

How do I know this?

Because that's how life goes.

And while I'm not attached to the outcome, I do hope this book ends up the way I know my life will: a beautiful masterpiece.

And how do I know that my life will be a beautiful masterpiece?

Because that's what love does. It makes anything, everything, beautiful.

And right now …

I am in love.

Having now finished the book I set out to write, I can see that there is a truth in these words, far more profound than I had the capacity to realize at the time.

I truly had no idea what would actually unfold, where this journey would take me, and that was a good thing. For had I known what the journey held—the depth, the intensity, the highs and lows—I might have been tempted to shrink away.

Before writing this book, and before the experience that catalyzed it, I had spent years in unfulfilling relationships, never allowing myself to be fully seen for fear of rejection, intimacy, the list goes on. I chose "safe" relationships—relationships that didn't require me to truly commit or open up, but instead allowed me to stay small and justify my convenient excuse for not going all in: "it would never work out—they aren't the one."

That story, I now see, was not the evidence I thought it was ... but actually the cause. I realized that I was the common denominator, and that the story I was telling myself was simply a projection of my own inner stories that I had deemed too uncomfortable to face head-on.

But after a lot of therapy, healing work, sacred plant medicine journeys, and many, many tears, I met myself as a new person. Fear had been replaced with peace. The flaws I perceived in others, and in myself, had been replaced with wholeness. And I came to realize that every past relationship had one thing in common: things left unsaid.

Learning that fear was the root of why I kept things inside instead of fully opening up and speaking the truest words I knew how—no matter how vulnerable—was a revelation. And when I committed to doing it properly, something beautiful happened...

I heard a whisper.

Life, God, whispering directly to my soul. Opening doors and extending invitations for me to enter through.

And when I committed to following that whisper, no matter the cost, two things happened: First, I experienced a new relationship in a way that I hadn't ever experienced a relationship before, and, second, these poems came to me.

The poems in this book flowed freely—after not having written a poem since my school days. Every one of them was a gift, allowing me to share what I was feeling, and also to learn from what I was experiencing. This whisper, Life, started to teach me through these poems.

This book *is* a love story. It is the story of two people, called on a Hero's Journey, invited to live in love, their responses being their own.

And now, I invite you to see yourself in these poems.

Let them whisper something to you.

See them as love notes sent from Life ...

and let that love make you a masterpiece.

The First Letter

Dear future wife,

I know it may seem strange to be writing you this letter before we've even met but I'm trusting that it will make sense to you by the time you're done reading it.

I've found that the same could be said for my entire life. No matter what challenges have come my way, things always seem to end up precisely the way they should.

An interesting thing happened recently. The sort of thing that, when it happens to you, you don't share it out loud with just anybody. The sort of thing that others might possibly think you're crazy for saying. The sort of thing that even you might just be tempted to think you were crazy for saying... except for the fact that it happened to you. And you know it was real because instead of making you feel crazy, it brings everything in your life and the world into crystal clear focus, and it brings you peace. Yes, right now, I feel an immense amount of peace. The kind of peace that says everything is unfolding exactly as it should.

Here's what happened:

I heard a whisper.

Not a whisper like when my adorable son is talking in his sleep. Not a whisper like when my daughter is trying to avoid answering the question that I've asked her that she really doesn't like. And not the kind of whisper that one might think they need medication to fix something in their brain.

No, this whisper was different. It was a quiet, gentle whisper - to my heart as much as it was to my mind - calling me to something.

An invitation…

And I answered.

I won't overload you with all the details of exactly what happened and how it unfolded - there will be plenty of time for that, trust me - but for now, just know that it brought me to this beautiful place where I am right now, writing you this letter.

And I intend to follow this whisper wherever it leads.

And, to be transparent, this isn't the only time I've heard this whisper calling me to something in life. I've felt its gentle invitation before - and sometimes I've followed - but eventually, I always found a way to retreat. Some fear, some story of my own inadequacy, some excuse got in the way and I shrunk from that invitation.

But this time was different.

This time I knew I didn't want to experience the shame and humiliation of letting myself down. Or letting you down. I didn't want to settle for being the kind of man who shrinks from what Life is calling him to do. This time I committed to following that voice, no matter the cost. Even if it meant being ridiculed, misunderstood, or even losing everything I once thought was important. I committed to honoring that whisper, even if it meant my life…

And then something broke. Something broke open in the most wonderful way. As if clouds parted from an eternal overcast, and the light finally shone in.

And that brought me to the mountain.

And on that mountain is where these poems first came through, as if they were a gift from Life itself.

My love, I wrote these poems for you.

I look forward to reading every one of them to you while staring into your eyes and sharing all of the details of this beautiful journey that has prepared me for you.

With love,

Joseph

Surrender Beckons

"Tell me something beautiful,"
she said.

"Surrender beckons,"
was all he replied.

And the world was never the same.

How is it possible
>   that one can be the spark
>   the kindling
>   the flame
>   the ember
>   and the fire
>   that warms my soul and
>   burns within my heart
>   yet also be the
>   one I yearn to share
>   its warmth with?

For that, my love,
>   is what you have become
>   to me.

The Spark

Why do I yearn to
    be seen by others?
    To be held in a place
    of significance by
    those I know not?
When all I need is to
    be seen by you,
    my love.
Is it because I do not
    see myself?
How silly.
    Let that stop this instant
    that love may flow
    and yearning cease
      left, only
        peace.

To Be Seen

Deep within me
    are all the
    fears, the
    unhealed hurt, the
    tears not cried, the
    words not spoken, the
    pain unfelt, the
    truth not embraced

that keep me living small;
that cause the waters of
my soul
    to sit stagnantly;
that slow the unfolding
    of God's grand purposes.

I wish to crack them open
every last one

to make room for you,
    my love.
Let us jump in
and sail these moving
waters together.

Moving Waters

Crack me open.
    Loosen my relentless,
    yet futile, grip
and take away from me
    all that I would hold, carry
    to burden my soul.

Steal it from me
    as a cunning thief,
    that I may not notice
    the act,
    until it's too late and
the burden is already lifted

and left behind
is only room for love.

                                        Crack Me Open

My soul is on a journey,
    won't you come along?

Join me,
    though I know not
    where it leads.

    Only that it will
    be perfect

    as long as you are
    by my side.

Let's be found,
    getting lost together

in perfect union,
with the Mapmaker Divine.

Lost Together

The great and grand
   purposes of God

      are only to be felt,
         seen,
         understood,
         enjoyed,
      by those who trust
         enough
         to jump in with both
         feet

         and let the divine wind
      carry them
         wherever it would
         take them.

                                                      Wind

Why do we seek to
find in others
what the divine
has already
placed in us?

Because two are
better than one,

and the union of
two trusting,
    surrendering souls

becomes a bigger one
than I was
    before you came along.

Two Are Better

I don't know if you
        understand this, but

I am in love with you
        and I never
        want to
        step out.

It doesn't matter one iota
        how you look,
        the state of your hair,
        what you bring.

Just that you stand here
        in this pool of love
        with me,

and never let either
of us get out.

                                        Pool of Love

I could make you
a promise,
and I probably will,

but I already made it
the instant I met
    you
and even before:

To love you always,
in the way you've made me
feel love myself.

It's perfect.

As is my promise,
it shall never change.

It just breathes.

The Promise

I found a rock
and stepped on it—

it pushed into the
       ground.

The dirt yielded,
the stone did not.

Both are strength:

different
but partners
in the same
journey to perfection.

Like you and me.

                                        Both Are Strength

Surrender is the
sweetest song,
for when we
sing,

we learn
that Life will catch us
and carry us
to our greatness

our destiny.

Surrender

We are all but
    beasts,

simply surviving.

Until we breathe in
    the divine and
    let Life do something
    beautiful with us.

Beasts

So I had an idea!

      Let's ignore caution
      embrace the risk

and forget about

what could go wrong—

      for the sake of
      what might go right.

Let's stay here.

An Idea

Answering the Call

"Yes, let's stay here,"
was her peaceful reply.

I've never understood
falling in love as if it were a pit,
or a force beyond one's control.

I've understood it to be a verb,
a choice we make,
actions we take.

Though now I see,
since you came along,
I am swimming in love
like a fish in water:

It is all it knows.
It never leaves it.
And it is the medium
through which it moves,
and lives, and how
it does any and every thing.

For these are my days—
I am swimming in love.
And even the mundane has new life,
for it is awakened by this love I am in.

And it is what moves me
from place to place,
from thought to thought,
from breath to breath,

and illumines everything anew.

I am in love with you.

Let's stay here.

Swimming

We are all
echoes of love

spoken from the
Divine.

Echoes

What if my demons
    want to eat me?
    Monsters that they are.

Let them.

I am eternal—
    and they are illusion.

If they consume me,
    they will disappear.

    Bye-bye for now,
    thanks for the
      memories.

My Demons

Lying still
in the silence
of your bedroom,

nothing between us
but the proof of my love.

My head on your chest—
the most beautiful sound
I've ever heard:

your heart drumming
a song of love
in through my ears

and straight into my heart,
where it sings along.

Somehow,
it already knows the words.

The Proof of My Love

Let me worship at
the altar of your body.

Drink your holy water.

Be cleansed by your loving embrace.

For I desire to offer myself
as a sacrifice in
eternal devotion
to you.

Altar

Every day
I am as a knight,
laying at your feet
my sword and my armor
in complete devotion to you.

To worship the divine feminine
through loyalty to you.

I honor you in every breath;
my devotion
is never far from me.

Knight

Sometimes it's
"I'm happy to be here"
"I've got your back no matter what"
"I'm terrified, don't let me go"
"You're my perfect match"
"I'm so proud of you"
"I'm utterly devoted to you"
or simply
"I hope you feel my love."

Regardless of the reason—
and for all of these
and so many more
yet to come—

I want to hold your hand
until the moment
I leave this earth.

No Matter the Reason

I'm sorry,

but if I go
before you do,

I've asked them to
amputate your hand

so I can be buried
with my fingers
intertwined with yours

forever.

Your Hand

I never thought I would be the person
to struggle with words;

to say or ask the right things
when I'm around you.

But hey—
being an imperfect man
in the presence of the perfect woman

can be a lot of pressure sometimes.

And even though I don't always
use the right words to
make you feel loved and seen,

one thing is for certain:

I love you.
I see you.

So when you think I'm too preoccupied
and you feel like I'm not giving
you the attention you deserve,

what I'm actually doing is taking notes.

And here's what I see:

Beauty.
Strength.
Virtue.
Faith.
Courage.
Love.

Perfection.

I See You

Being present
is life in color.

Disconnected
is black and white.

It's Higher and
Lower Nature.

If you aren't connected to who you really are
you'll feel disconnected and lacking.

And probably try to blame it on someone else
or the world around you.

Being Present

Conflict is only seeing
part of the picture.

When we see clearly—
conflict dissolves.
The product of truth
is wholeness, unity.

Whatever the issue,
if we see two opposing sides,
we don't yet see clearly.

Seek truth, find wholeness.

Conflict

Happiness is not
getting what
we want.

It's loving what
we have.

The only truth you need
to set you free,
is right here,
right now.

Let's stay here.

Happiness Is Here

Love is not a feeling.

Love is a lens
through which we see
ourselves,
others,
the world.

It's not a feeling,
but a lens that creates our feelings.

It's not a verb,
but a lens that inspires our actions.

It's not what happens between two people,
but the lens that makes beautiful things possible.

It's not a miracle,
but this lens, when chosen, helps us see the beauty and magic we previously
took for granted.

Let us choose love.

The Lens

Our love is like a plant:

You are the sunshine,
I am the rain.

If only one of us shows up,
it gets scorched
or flooded.

But if we both show up,
even if we have to take turns,
it grows.

Taking Turns

Sometimes
I wonder if you think
I write these sweet poems
and say and do the things I do
because I see you as a magical unicorn
and you give me special feelings
I've never felt before.

Nonsense.

I do it because that's
how relationships work:
You get what you give.

And I'm trying to build
something magical
with you.

And so,
with each word,
with each stroke of the pen,
I invest.
I build.

Unicorn

There are times we feel connected, whole.
And then there are times we are conflicted.

Life is a dance between choosing.
Life, or death.
Love, or emptiness.
(Truth, or the lie.)

In which do you dwell?
And in which would you like to be?

Dwelling

Some are comfortable
with easy.

Not me.

Easy is the path to
ordinary.

Give me the hard path.
Give me adversity.

What I want to
create with you

lies far beyond
the reach of mere
mortals resigned to the
easy route.

Will you walk the hard
path with me?

The Hard Path

Take the risk.
Exercise courage.
Be brave.
Have faith.

Even if you fail marvelously,

you'll be better
by the act.

Just trust.

Life has you.

Especially when
you trust
enough
to jump.

Trust

The Fork in the Road

It wasn't so much that
either of them had changed,

but perhaps one of them
stopped nurturing the seed of faith

that Love had planted in their heart.

He was writing love poems.

She was making exit plans.

Writing Poems

I can keep showing up,

all in.

All I need is for you to say
that you give a shit,
that you're trying,
that you want it.

Anything

instead of staying silent.

The goddamn silence
is killing us.

Deadly Silence

"I'm not sure I see the value
of being in a relationship."

What the actual fuck?

How does someone so brilliant
not see all of life pointing
to the truth that we are
meant to live in connection
with one another?

That the height of this
human experience is found
in sharing it with someone
we can love unreservedly?

Fear,
or lies.

Those are the only explanations.

Fear, or Lies?

Was it too much to expect
that you would call me back
like you said you would?

At the very least I thought
you might apologize
for wasting my time.

But instead you ran and hid,
seeking some false
promise of protection.

Do you not see the sheer
immensity of your greatness?

You don't need to shrink from
anything,
let alone telling the truth.

Or am I simply an idiot
for seeing something that
wasn't there?

Too Much to Ask

I would have gladly
taken a bullet
to assure you of
my love…

If only you had
let me know

that you ever,
even for a moment,
doubted.

If Only

It was real—
you felt it.

How you could dissociate
so quickly would baffle me

if it weren't for the fact
that now I have to do
the same just to survive.

The only difference is that
I stayed in long enough
to feel the pain
and let it purify me

and you did it preemptively,
running away from some imaginary
fear—leaving me to deal with
it for both of us.

And you missed the wisdom
that is only found through
suffering, and the peace
of staying all in,
no matter the cost.

The Difference

Anyone I speak to
and share the plain facts of what happened
agrees
that no caring human being,
with even an ounce of empathy,
would do what you did to me.

But still I give you the benefit of the doubt.

Despite the confusion,
and the anguish,
and the pain,

still I trust you—

that you had a noble reason
even if I didn't see it, or understand.

I can't help but trust you.

Because I've seen your essence,
I know that beneath everything
I can't wrap my head around,

you are Love.

Perhaps I should have trusted you a little more.

And perhaps I should have trusted myself more.

And instead of leaning on you,
believing that you would support me,

I should have surrendered,
and found that support within.

For I, too,
am Love.

And love is what
makes us whole.

Your Essence

If you didn't need the love
I had to offer you

then you are definitely
out of my league

and we are better off apart.

Because I'm still the kind of person
who is made better
when there is love around me

and I have no desire
to change that.

If wanting someone to
share love with
and be open to
and build dreams with
makes me needy

then I never want to be whole.

Needy

The loneliest I felt
was not when
I was
alone,
but when
the person
who said they were my partner
couldn't be bothered
to tell me the truth.

The truth would have been easy,
no matter how harsh.

But how do I forgive
the silence?

The Loneliest

I carry a lot of pain.
It's heavy,
But it keeps me grounded.

At least it feels that way.

But it seems to be
bringing the past
to the present moment.

It's a lens
that skews the perception
of anything I'm seeing.

Like weeds, a heavy history,
tangling itself with today.

Why can't I let it go?
Why can't I break free?
What am I missing?

I know I'm asking the
wrong questions.

And I know that there's
no liberation to be found
in believing a lie.

And I know there's no room
to receive anything new
when I'm clinging to something that isn't there.

But the gap between
who I feel I am,
and the results in my life,
haunts me so much,

I can't help but feel despair,
because the answers to
even the right questions
elude me

                                          Burdened.

You said that you wanted
someone who would know you—

who would take the time
to listen
and see you truly at the depth
of who you are.

And now it seems clear
the things we want
from others

are so often the things
we refuse to give ourselves.

How telling that the beautiful truth
you spoke, which sparked the fire
of our love for each other,

"Someone can only meet you
        as deep as they've met themselves,"

would also be the bitter truth
responsible for its demise.

The Truth You Spoke

I would have gladly held space
for you to spew vitriol and anger at me.

I was silently screaming to know you.

I was ready to receive it
from the first moment you said
you wanted to be seen.

Not just the pretty,
or the comfortable,

but all of you.

Real,
raw,
vulnerable,
open.

To sit beside you and
experience everything with you:

The doubt.
The uncertainty.
The pain.
The triumph.

To ride every single up and down,
not just the even plains or the pretty views.

I'm not afraid of the mess, because
I know what's on the other side.

Why did you stay silent,
when I was begging to give you
the one thing you said you wanted most?

Ready to Receive

It wasn't that I wanted you
to "meet me on my level,"
like you said.

I just thought we could
stay where we were
when we said,

"Let's stay here."

I Thought We Could Stay

The real difference
in how we approached
this relationship
is that when I had
a grievance,
I brought it up as it happened
and aired it immediately
in hopes that we could resolve it
so it would make us stronger.
And when you had a grievance
you kept it inside
and let it become
a wedge, turning into
resentment,
so you could feel justified
in protecting yourself
from something that
only wanted
to love you
and make you
whole.

Grievances

May I never
be as reckless
with someone's heart,
or their childrens',
as you were
with ours.

For the Love of the Children

It would hurt to imagine you
with someone new.

To imagine you
moving on
and enjoying the beautiful things
we've pictured together,
without me.

It would hurt to realize
that all those possibilities—
so rich,
so beautiful—
were dead and gone,
never to come back again.

It would hurt to imagine
that you had let me go,
and didn't have a place for me
in your heart anymore.

But it would be enough to remember
the moments we shared,
the love we felt,

and the possibility that my love
helped you see in yourself
what I so clearly saw from the beginning:

Beauty.
Love.
Courage.
Perfection.

Someone New

I don't regret one
single thing about us

except maybe my assumption
that you meant what you said.

Regrets

We lived in two different worlds.

You just liked to come and visit me
in mine every once in a while.

And I just hoped you'd want to stay.

But saying "let's stay here"
is a futile wish

when someone is simply
passing through.

The only things that can be
relied upon without fail

are the things that
never change.

And that list is small:

Truth. Love.

Two Different Worlds

Walking the Path Alone

"I'm confused, conflicted,
and I'm not sure I can do this,"
she confessed.

Although he would have found the
message much easier to understand
had she actually used her words,
instead of keeping it inside.

It took him months to
decipher the confession
simply from her conflicted behavior.

I keep wanting life to give
me the perfect words

to bring you back to me,

back to this space
we shared together,

back to this pool of love,
where I now stand

alone.

This Pool

I carved you love letters into stone
you wrote yours in the sand.

When the waves of life
came upon us

yours washed away,
mine were only polished.

But now I have them still
long after you've let me go.

Love is not meant to be
a heavy burden to carry.

What did I do wrong?

Sand and Stone

You had a taste,

a sample of the
beauty and splendor
in this world of love,

and I'm grieving
that you didn't want
to feast with me

forever.

The Feast

We weren't on different levels.

We were equal in every way.

Our strengths a liberating gift to the other

to bring balance,

a beautiful harmony.

No, we weren't on different levels.

But maybe you just didn't see the
beauty of your own
greatness

reflecting in me

as I saw mine
in you.

Equals

I don't want to let you go—

I want you back.

I gave myself to you so fully,
so completely—

my heart was yours.

I have never opened myself up
to hurt so much
in trusting you
and surrendering to you
as I did.

And I don't regret it.

But I wish we could go back,
to when we both
chose love.

When We Both Chose Love

I'm sorry that I am an imperfect human being

and I relied on you for strength sometimes
and hoped that you would
fill needs when I was
running low.

I didn't mean to burden you.

I suppose I could have
let God do that stuff.

But the messiness of life
is part of what makes
it all so beautiful.

And I cherished the idea
that we were in this
wonderful, messy thing
together.

Imperfect

I thought my invitation
would be enough,
seeing us as equals.

You expect me to take
the lead, to prove that
I meant what I said.

I can't decide
who failed who.

Who Failed Who

How could the catalyst not know
the true sense of beauty,
the sheer magnitude of magnificence,
the purity of worship.

A lifetime of devotion
couldn't communicate
the depth of love
in my soul for you.

But in your forsaking,
your act of surrender,
in giving up the most sacred,
in leaving the promised land

—laying down your life;
an unintentional messiah—

you birthed something
so beautiful,
a legacy
never to be forgotten.

I only wish you
were here to taste it,
and share its
splendor with me
forever.

The Catalyst

Looking back,
the only wish I'd make

would be for you
to have felt
as safe with me,

as I felt with you.

My Only Wish

I was never asking for certainty,
just commitment.

Just as Peter had no certainty
he'd walk on water,

but still risked getting wet
and stepped out of the boat.

It's commitment that unlocks the miracle,
there's no need for certainty.

Commitment

I had no desire to point fingers,
find fault, or pass judgment of any kind,

because if you kept things left unsaid
I know you were already doing
those things to yourself.

There is no reason to fear the truth whatsoever,
and doing so only reveals
that we believe the lie,
the illusion of our separateness.

Because speaking the truth
—no matter how threatening to our ego—
is the exact path to our liberation,
and how we return to our Higher Nature.

That was my commitment all along;
I'm sorry that I didn't realize
it was no longer yours, and
I projected mine onto you.

Things Left Unsaid

You said you didn't want to hurt me,
that you never intended
for that to happen.

I believe you.

Hurting others is never
an intention of the heart;

it's always a byproduct of
trying to protect ourselves
from something that isn't real.

That's why speaking the truth
is so important: Doing so dispels untruths
and imbues us with power to surrender the lies.

When we don't heal our wounds,
we bleed on people who didn't cut us.

I hope you know I was
never afraid of the blood

and was patient enough
to hold space

for as long as it took
for you to heal them all.

Never Afraid

It doesn't matter how thrilling,

if you ride a roller coaster for long enough,
in the end it's just a merry-go-round.

I loved the ups and downs,
but only because I thought
we were on a road
leading somewhere beautiful.

As soon as I saw that you
just wanted to go in circles,

I had to get off the ride.

I'm here for a purpose,
not just amusement.

Roller Coaster

I was willing to take a bullet for you.

But when I saw
that you weren't even
on the battlefield,

I knew the only sane move
was to remove myself
from the line of fire.

Line of Fire

Out of the virtue of commitment

I stayed with someone who
couldn't even articulate
any value to being
in a relationship,

never mind the
beautiful toil of
getting their hands dirty
in the commitment of living in one.

I'll own that.

I am responsible,
for I was the one who
—wanting so deeply for it to be you—
sacrificed my values,

when what I really wanted
was someone who sees
that who and how they choose to love
can be the very means to their
salvation and enlightenment
in this world.

Because that person
would not have shied away
from the hard work…
or at the very least,
they would have
told the truth.

Lesson learned.

Virtue and Work

You said that you were upset that I
pointed out the difference between
when you showed up in your

Higher Nature and your Lower.

Or was it simply that you didn't
like seeing it?

The difference between the two
was stark,
the sign of a mind at conflict with itself.
A psyche at odds with its spirit.

Or were you just upset that I noticed?

Did you fear that my own
standards of integrity

would mean you weren't good enough?

And so you simply preempted
the painful end you predicted?

How sad.

I would have loved you through it all,
until you saw the wholeness in you
that I saw from the very beginning.

Through It All

The stories you told me
post-mortem were bullshit.

Miles away from the
teary-eyed truths you
vulnerably shared
from your best Self.

But I understand why…

You were no longer there.

How silly of me to think
my love could keep you there

when you had no interest
in facing the shame or
confronting the fears
that kept you away.

No Longer There

Some day
I hope
you see

that I was
not trying
to fight you.

I was trying
to fight *for* you.

The Beautiful Fight

I noticed that you
didn't have to ask
why my energy shifted.

I guess you finally
put it together
that I know
the truth.

Funny thing is, I knew all along.

Like I said,
I could have held space
for you to share anything.

All you needed to do was lean in…

But shame has a way of
holding us back,
and weighing us down.

Don't worry,
I'll leave that burden with you.

I know better than to let that
affect my self-worth.

Leave It with You

When our minds are clear,
we choose only that
which serves our evolution.

When our hearts are pure,
we choose only that
which to others is a contribution.

When We're Clear

It was our anniversary.

The kids and I were back at the place
where it all began.

But we weren't ready
to say goodbye.

We decided to keep you
as a happy memory

and hold on to the possibilities
for just a little while longer

in case you came back to us.

Or perhaps so we could muster
the courage to finally
let you go.

Our Anniversary

If this were to be the last poem
that I would ever write,

what would I want to say?

Is there a swan song,
a message so profound,
that I could leave this world,
and you,
feeling whole and complete,
and that nothing had been left unsaid?

Yes.

Everything is exactly as it should be,
and everything is right on time.

Though I had a moment of believing the lie,
the truth remains:

I'm staying here.

The Last Poem

Letting Go

When she finally left,
with only empty space in her wake,

he realized that sometimes things
remove themselves from our lives

because we are growing,
and we need the space to bloom.

I'm still carrying
you with me.

In my active thoughts,
my longings,
my aspirations
and dreams,
my passionate fantasies…

I have to let you go.

You're taking up

space.

Taking Up Space

If you don't want
to step up,
or lean in,

then please
step down,
get out.

I have no interest
in a half-lived life.

In/Out

This is healing—
this, feeling.
This, living it.
This, breathing it in
and experiencing everything
so intensely.

It's vivid.

Why some are content
to live their empty lives
baffles me.

Feel something, dammit.

This, Feeling

You have to take all
your hopes and dreams,
your deepest desires,
your secret wishes,

and place them on
the sacrificial altar
and surrender them to the Divine

or you'll never
find freedom

or feel
true love.

Surrender All

Breathe.

Notice it deeply,
feel every sensation.

Get present to everything
that happens inside
your body.

Feel the life
sustaining you,

the same life
sustaining all creation,

and see clearly
that it is

love.

Breathe

There is wisdom that can only
be found in suffering.

But you have to endure;

you have to abide
to sit with it
to feel it all
go deep
not shy away

until the pain turns into peace
and the heart is open enough
to let truth enter it
and fill you with love.

Don't give up—let the pain
take you somewhere
beautiful.

Beautiful Wisdom

I see you.

You are beautiful.

There is love flowing so deeply
within you

that it cannot be separated
from you—

it sustains you.

And in trusting it,
surrendering to
its loving embrace,

we see clearly.

We see truth.

We see ourselves.

Beautiful

It is true that "love is not love which
alters when it alteration finds."
And so it is true that my love for you is constant,
even though I have to let you go.

This love,
it is not longing (though long for you, I certainly did)
it is not desire (though desiring you, I certainly did)
it is not attachment (though close to you, I certainly felt).

This love,
it is acceptance
it is surrender
it is celebrating you

This love
is embracing you fully for who you are,
though I'll never hold you again.

                                                        This Love

* Thanks to William Shakespeare's Sonnet 116

There are moments that
I fear missing you

but then I remember
that if life brought
you to me back then

—an unexpected gift of grace—

then I have nothing to fear
for the future

considering how much
of a better version
of myself
I am today

because of you.

Because of You

If you think
that somehow
I don't still love you,
even after all that has happened,

then it is a certain impossibility
that you ever understood
the depth of my love for you.

"Unconditional" and "undying"
mean precisely that.

Every act was out of devotion
to the vision we shared,

and if you somehow interpreted
my feedback as criticism,

then you certainly didn't understand
my commitment to creating
the most beautiful masterpiece
of a relationship together—

because only love, not disdain,
is willing to travel that path.

Impossible

Love is not afraid of conflict.

Love will bring
The lies
And errors
And offer them to the light,

Where they can die
The death they deserve.

Boldly and courageously
Will love examine
Every story
Every feeling
Every thought

And humbly surrender them
On the altar of truth,

Until only purity remains.

No, love need not fear the conflict
that arises in our relationships,
For it is only the means
Of surrendering the war within ourselves,
And we achieve that sweet victory of peace
The moment we value truth more than our shadow.

For it is only when we see clearly
That we finally understand
The truth of love–
The unthreatenable beauty of our perfection–
That our illusions
Attempt to obscure.

The Beautiful Conflict

The silence

is bliss
when we are partnered with Life;

our sanctuary
our haven
our teacher
our healer
our solace.

And it is terror when we
are separated from the
truth of who we are.

So we avoid it,
distracting and numbing,
fearing the exact thing

that will set us
free.

The Silence

I wanted to say hello,
to speak to you,
to tell you how beautiful you are.

But I waited,
hoping you would
reach out to me,

thinking it was you…

not realizing that
what I wanted most

was just waiting
inside of me

to be found,
to be seen,
to be honored.

What I Wanted Most

To love deeply

to live richly
to speak truthfully
to feel vividly

this is success

and how much sweeter it is
to share it
with you.

Success

I miss you.

But only when I forget

that everything

you gave me,

showed me,

was simply a reflection

of the divine spark within me,

and an expression

of that timeless love

which sustains

us all.

Reflection

There is a big difference between
not feeling it anymore
and healing it.

I don't want to shy away from anything
in this life, not one
single painful experience,

but courageously face it.

Stare it down
until it gives way
and I am made whole.

Bloodied,
battered,
bruised,

but stronger,
more perfect.

Healing

In a period where I had all uncertainty,
I was looking to create certainty
where I wanted it most:

with you.

But true confidence is living with uncertainty.

And I've learned that
trying to build something
with the wrong materials

is not only a futile endeavor,
it's delusion of the sweetest flavor,
with the most bitter of aftertastes.

The Myth of Certainty

Just let it all go.

Throw everything into
the arms of the Divine

and let the river of life
take you where it will.

It knows a better path
than you'll ever discover
on your own.

Trust it.

Let it take you on a journey of love,
and teach you truth;

the kind that is only found
in surrender.

A Better Path

The Treasure

"For when I saw
that you are me,
and I am you,
all enmity dissolved
forever,"

he whispered as he let her go.

When my heart broke
I learned that
a heart can break open
or break closed.

And when mine broke open
it made space for what
I had been seeking
all along.

And in surrendering to the pain
I found that it was love
entering in,
cleansing my soul,
bringing peace.

How a Heart Breaks

In the depth
of my agony

I found
a seed

preserved by
the pressure,
so tightly
bound,

ready to bloom

the instant
I let go,

and let
peace flow,

and chose
to nourish
that seed

to life.

The Depth

All the things I wanted from you:

commitment,
devotion,
connection,
communion,

to be all in...

I see now
were a reflection
of what Life wanted
from me.

In breaking my heart,
you made room for me
to find what it was that I
truly seeking:

God.

What I Was Seeking

At the root of nearly every origin story,
in the epic battle between light and dark,
there is:

an impulse to control others, or
a choice to honor free will,
and to extend an invitation
to walk in one's Higher Self.

To hold space for others—
instead of manipulating them—
requires

faith,
patience,
surrender,
love,

and the risk that we might
be hurt in the process.

But it is what calls forth
the greatness from within,
both in ourselves

and also in those for whom we hold space
to be seen for who they are—
especially if they haven't taken the time
to really see themselves—
and allow them to confront
their nature: who they are, their Divine Essence,
and how aligned their behavior is with that True Self.

Hold Space

Feeling superior,
or inferior,
is a sign of disconnection:

a reminder that
we are unplugged
from our true nature.

When we see clearly,
we experience connection,

seeing all as equals;

we perceive no threat,
and offer only contribution.

Unplugged

When I am tempted to focus
on the behavior of others,
may I be reminded that they
are a gift to reflect
what I have yet to see within.

When I am inclined to focus on
what I am not getting, or
what I feel I am lacking,
may I be reminded to go and give
from the Everlasting Supply
to others.

May I bring light,
by sitting in peace
with the darkness.

May I bring joy,
by sitting in truth
with those who grieve.

May I wholly surrender to Life,
that all illusion may be dispelled.

Teach me how to love.

Teach Me How to Love

Pain will speak to you if you let it.
It will show you wisdom if you sit with it.
It will heal you if you are patient.
If you learn to love it, it will make you whole.

And when you've made your peace with it,
and received all its gifts,
it will let you let it go.

Pain

There is a fear
at the edge of surrender,

that if embraced,
would mock
the things of purity,
and the Divine itself.

It would push away
the very thing we want the most,

just to avoid the shame
of recognizing our own
retreat.

When all we needed to do
to stay standing in that pool of love

was surrender even that fear
and trust that God would
make us whole.

Edge of Surrender

Your assumptions
will kill you,

unless you let
their reflections
heal you.

Either way,
they'll have their
way with you
in the end.

Assumptions

When we don't
heal the wounds
of the heart,

our minds will step in
to cover them with scars
in the form of stories
designed to protect.

But the cost is that
we lose some depth,
a capacity to feel,
and life loses a degree of vividness.

Yet, if we summon the courage
to pull off those scars,
we still have to face the original wounds—
from slavery to the desert—
before we can reach the promised land;
the place of union,
where we return to oneness
with the divine within our hearts–

the very kingdom of heaven
our protective stories were
obstructing us from,
simply because we feared a little pain,

which fear was only
caused by believing
an untrue story
to begin with.

The Courage To Heal

The courageous,
the ones who create beauty
and have turned life
into a living masterpiece

have mastered one lesson:
Fear is the reason to act,
to follow the gentle nudge that brings us to the precipice,
and to dive all in,
without reservation.

To walk on water
and behold the miracle within

while the weak
see fear and shy away

and trade in the miracle, hoping
to settle for comfort
instead.

But in the end,
their empty, desperate
lives are marked
only by loneliness
and regret.

Yet both are designed to bring us to our true selves.
To show us the end
for which we are striving—
whether by confirmation
or by contrast.

And it all comes full circle the moment
we surrender and
lay it all on
the altar of Life.

The Living Masterpiece

You're in this world, not of it.
You don't have to participate.

Listen to your heart.

Your freedom lies in listening.
Let it lead you somewhere beautiful.
Let it set you free.

There is a whole world
of beauty and life
waiting for you,

but you have to accept
the invite.

You have to answer the call.

And you have to take the
step of faith.

Invitation

I crave physical connection.

I want to be held.
I want to feel safe.

But mostly, I want to be
reminded that I can
hold myself.

Healing is simply letting go
of the lie.

Rewriting the story
of what we think things mean
and replacing it with
something beautiful and true.

Beautiful Embrace

Seeking truth
is arguably
the most important
thing we can do.

Pursuing truth dispels illusion,
and the illusion
is the source of
all our suffering.

All pain and suffering, unfulfillment,
are rooted in believing things that aren't true.

Whether ideas,
or our own thoughts,

it is believing things
that disconnect us from Life,
that disconnect us from the inner whisper
that leads us on the peaceful path,
and that disconnect us
from the joy that comes

as we surrender
to the moving waters
of the divine flow.

Seeking Truth

The very things about others
that "trigger" us, or bother us,

are the very things we need
to purify our souls.

They are reflections of untruths
we believe within ourselves.

Seeing them as things in others
—instead of as in ourselves—

is proof that we have it backwards,
that we see it upside down,

as staring at the underside
of a tapestry.

And it is only when we can rise above
—where we belong—

by surrendering the sandbags of
false belief, resentment, or fear,

that we see clearly that
those reflections were trying to

show us the magnificence
of our true nature,

and purify our minds,
from the very things

—the lies we believed
about ourselves—

that we chose to keep it hidden.

The Tapestry

Conflict does not
happen
between people,

it happens
within them.

All conflict is
simply between
love and fear—

of choosing to shrink,
and hide from
the very thing our soul seeks,

or letting Life
lift us up,
and expand our
souls with light;

to find wholeness,
where before
we felt fractured,

for simply believing
the untrue
thought.

The Untrue Thought

Love is willing to walk a hard path,
not shy away from it.

For love knows there is
nothing to fear—

nothing real can ever be threatened.

Only our illusions ever perceive attack.

Love knows that pain only hurts
if you don't see the purpose,

that discomfort is simply our
lies clashing with the truth,

and that on the other side
of every difficult thing
we experience

is the seed of something so beautiful and profound

that if we could only see it now,
we'd embrace the pain with gratitude

and laugh at the thought
that we ever tried to hide.

Love Knows

Our minds will wrestle
to come up with stories
that help us make sense
of difficult situations—

it's the mind's survival instinct,
designed to protect us—

but true insight doesn't
come from the struggle,
it comes from surrender.

When we are ready
to lay down
our swords and shields,

and embrace truth,
instead of story,

Life will show us the beauty
that we somehow thought
we needed to protect ourselves from.

Let the struggle make you stronger,
but remember

that it's surrender
that makes you beautiful.

Wrestle

We've been in this place a thousand times.

But this time we are new.

Let's breathe.

Let's enjoy it.

Savor every single flavor that this moment brings.

This profound gift that life has given us.

Let us not take it for granted.

Let's stay here.

This Time

Coming Home

"Don't you see,"
Life whispered,

"I was always only ever trying
to show you who you are.
That beautiful gift,
that you deemed worthy of worship,
was simply a mirror."

First, there's the loneliness
of losing them.

Then, the loneliness
of realizing that you
were in love with someone
who was already checking out.

Next, love enters in
and heals you.

Enter, Love

You have to be willing
to dance with
your brokenness

before you can
truly understand
and embody
your wholeness.

Because what
you don't make
your peace with
makes your peace
impossible.

So sit with it,
feel it, heal it,

and let love make
you whole.

Dance

Life will show us who we are

when we are ready
to go all in—

to trust completely
that voice within

which speaks truth,
which whispers to our souls:

"You are right where you need to be."

It is only in trusting, so
fully that we could lay
down our lives,

that we see the magnificence
that is inside of us,
and feel the pure love
that is our very nature.

Who We Are

Every true act of beauty

is a love song to the divine;
a poem of devotion to the
highest good of all.

So sing.

Sing

Dear God,

this peace
this love
this perfection

—as I trust in you, and
you flow through me—

let's stay here.

Dear God

Look within
and see wholeness.

Find the healing that you seek,
the moment you surrender your will to Life
and let the peace flow
like healing rivers.

Let it wash over you,
and cleanse you.

Look Within

What if instead of trying to fix
the brokenness,
I could just appreciate its beauty?

What if instead of looking
for the lesson,
I could just let it find me?

It would know where I am
simply by following
the sounds of laughter.

And when it did arrive
it would have to find an opening
somewhere between my appointments
with peace and joy.

Calendar

I'm sorry that I projected my
own inadequacies onto you

and failed to appreciate you
the way that you deserve.

It wasn't that I didn't see you
for who you truly are.

It's because I was blinded by my own failings—
the stories about myself that weren't true—

that I ended up giving to you
the things I was trying to find myself.

Thank you for reminding me of
what I didn't see.

I only wish I had received
the message sooner,

so that I didn't let my own
unmet need for love

cause me to inadvertently
withhold mine from you.

Or at least so it seemed,
because even that
is a story without truth,

for Love gives us
exactly what we need,
when we need it,

and simply
calls us
to believe.

My Projections

However true it may be,
it feels too spiteful to say
that I'm better off
without you

unless I also say
that I'm better off
because
of you.

Thank you.

Better

The very gifts that God
gives us along our journey
to show us our worth,

He later asks for us to give back,
to see if we will trust Him
to show us that we
are worth even more.

Will you trust in the
truth of your own
magnificence?

And exercise the faith
required to claim
the gift waiting for you?

The Gift

I hope you know

that there is no version
of this story,

no possible ending,

in which I do not

love you unconditionally,

always and forever.

Unconditional

Love is not an easy path.

It is not for the cowards,

though it is precisely
what they need—

for love heals cowardice.

If only we could all have
the patience
to endure the fire

that burns away all our stories
that falsely give us reason
to fear in the first place.

Then love would prevail.

As it now does in my heart.

Not for Cowards

Loving.
Patient.
Forbearing.
Long-suffering.

I was willing to hold space
and be whatever you needed me to be

for you to be seen and know
how deeply you were loved,

trusting in the understanding that we
were in this together.

Partners.

But when I came to understand
that you changed your mind
—and voided our agreements—
without sharing that information
with me,

how you showed up was laid
on the scales of integrity
and found wanting.

Thank you for making it easy
to let you go.
I now have plenty of space
to let someone else into this pool of love,
where I stand ready to receive a true partner.

The Understanding

Everywhere we look,
if our eyes are open,
we can witness the ongoing
cycles of life and death.

Being present is to ride the
crest of waves of beginning
and ending:

the delicate balance of not
drifting to the future or
to the past,

but living with precision,
right where our breath is.

With each inhale
and exhale,

behold the whispered
name of God

and become partners
in creation

with Life itself.

Witness

Love is a refiner's fire,
and will consume anything
unlike itself,
in the end.

The only way
to not get burned
in the process
is to surrender the impurities
before the flame draws near.

Purify yourself,
that love may
simply warm you,
and light your path.

Refiner's Fire

Life will bring you back to me.

Perhaps not in the form
that I remember you,

but as I always
experienced you:

Love.

A New Form

This peace
this surrender
this love
this trusting

this knowledge

that life will enfold me in its loving arms
and also bring you all the love you deserve;

Let's stay here.

Let's Stay Here

The Final Letter

Dear future wife,

I'm imagining you reading this letter, and the image fills me with peace and brings a smile to my face. I've imagined this moment many times and for many different reasons. I feel connected to you. There isn't a day that goes by that I don't think of you with appreciation and gratitude. There isn't a day that I don't marvel at your beauty. And it isn't how you look, the state of your hair, or the gift of your physical body - no matter how much we may laugh that these things may be proof of how much God loves me - it is your essence. I see you. It is who you are that astounds me. I may not know all the details of your journey yet - I do look forward to you sharing them, though - but I do know who they have made you into. And that is where my attention is. It is your being that captivates me. Yes, there is beauty in the past - both in the triumph and the failures - but it is the present that I am concerned with. Who you are matters to me so much that I don't tend to dwell much on how you got there, just that you did.

I'm also hoping that if you've gotten this far, you've learned a few things about me. And while I know that you don't know all the details of how I got here (perhaps sharing all those stories is a project we can take on once we get settled into our little homestead together), I am trusting that what you've read has given you a glimpse into the essence of who I am: namely, what matters most to me in this life and the lens I use to interpret the world and our interactions.

But, for the sake of clear communication, I want to articulate a few things explicitly:

First, while I've been on my own, I've done my work. I've sat with every single thing that I've been through in this life. Every pain, every heartbreak, every failure, all the shame, the guilt, the fear, the trauma, the missed opportunities… every single thing that fell short of peace and perfection, and I've done the work on it. I've felt every feeling that needed to be felt. I've made every apology that needed to be made. I've cleaned up every single part of my life that was out of integrity. I did that work for myself. I

147

did that work for my children. And I did that work for you. I did it so that I can stand whole and complete, and at peace with my life. Every single part of it. As a consequence, I see myself clearly. I know exactly who I am. I've seen the divinity inside of me, as clear as one sees the sun on a summer afternoon, and I walk through this world experiencing myself as whole and complete, perfect as I am. A unique expression of the consciousness of Life, unfolding exactly as it should. And this is precisely how I see other people. I make no assumptions of brokenness. I see others as divine beings, worthy of love and respect, exactly as they are. I engage with them with a presupposition of wholeness, not the fracturedness that is experienced as we indulge the untrue stories of our shadow. As such, you may notice that I speak directly. I value truth and I speak to things as I see them.

Paradoxically, I also recognize that I'm a work in progress. While the essence of who I am is perfect, how I show up in this world, practically speaking, will fall far short. I'm going to mess up. I'm going to get things wrong. I'm going to make mistakes as I navigate being human. But the mistakes don't scare me. Being challenged when I'm missing the mark doesn't bother me one bit, and I won't shy away from conflict. In fact, I crave being called out when I'm not seeing something clearly. That's how I grow, no matter how uncomfortable… and I'm not afraid of discomfort. The only thing I fear (although fear isn't quite the right word) is remaining in ignorance. If I'm getting something wrong, I want to know about it. I want you to speak to it, so I can look at it and let it go. I want to look at all of my shortcomings because I can hold space for them with love and compassion but also be ruthless enough to tell the truth. Making mistakes doesn't shake the way that I see myself, it's simply the process of letting go of all that is untrue about who I truly am.

I also want to be clear about a few things about you:

I see you. I have witnessed your perfection, and I know who you are. I have beheld your true nature and see you as the divine queen that you are. But that doesn't mean I'm putting you on a pedestal. I see you clearly. And I understand that while you are whole and complete, perfect as you are, you are also paradoxically a work in progress. A perfect rose, still unfolding. As such, your imperfections don't frighten me in the slightest. I lovingly see and embrace your imperfections and am not threatened by them. I can witness them with love and compassion, and if I speak to them, it doesn't negate the truth of your essence.

148

Truth is our ally, not our nemesis. The only thing required for us to make this relationship into a masterpiece is a profound capacity for telling the truth. I want you to tell the truth about what you are experiencing, no matter how uncomfortable, and to lean into it so that we can share in this journey as true partners. I will hold space for you, but the truly courageous step - speaking the truest words you know how - is yours and yours alone. Know that there is always room for the truth here. I would far rather have the truth - whether it's about you, your perception of me, whatever - than to hide it in the shadows to fester. Because that's where the wedges grow. I am fully committed to seeing the truth, and so I hope you are fully committed to speaking it.

Lastly, there is room for you here. All of you. The perfect divine essence of who you are in your true nature, as well as the beautiful shortcomings you make in this human experience. And if you ever find yourself willing to look at your shortcomings, I will hold up the mirror of your perfection so we can laugh at the untrue stories together.

One more thing I can almost guarantee: our union will bring up our shit. That's what relationships do. When we feel love, and its healing power brings safety into our bodies, the old shit we haven't dealt with starts to bubble up… because it wants to be seen and loved and healed. It's not the stuff that comes up that compromises relationships; it's our unwillingness to put that stuff on the table that poisons them. Let's not shy away from those gifts. Let's stay here and dig into what comes up. Let's let this love be a refiner's fire and purify our souls, that we may cast off all the untruths that are unworthy of this beautiful love.

And so,
When you're ready,
I'll be here.

I'll be here, standing in this pool of love. Ready to receive you, my Queen… Where I have been standing all along, as promised, from the beginning.

Love, Joseph

"Even after all this time
the Sun never
says to the Earth,
"You owe me."

Look what happens
with a love like that,
it lights the whole sky."

- Hafiz

Afterword

Before I even finished compiling this book, or even writing/receiving all of these poems, I penned these words to end the book:

> *"Let's stay here" is a call to the present moment.*
>
> *It is an invitation to surrender, to experience the only thing that's real: this moment, exactly as it is. To let go of our attachments, our aversions. To let go of our stories of what things mean. To let go of the need to make sense of it all, or even any of it, and just embrace the truth: things are exactly as they are.*
>
> *Arguing with reality is a futile endeavor, and a sure way to relinquish our peace.*
>
> *Loving what is, breathing in the moment and seeing the good life right where we are.*

That is the call: Let's stay here.

It seemed complete, and I believe these words are true and powerful. But now I see they are also only part of the picture.

While one might walk away from this book feeling they've read a story of two lovers who diverged when life's inevitable challenges arose, it is my hope that they'll come away with something more—something that might even challenge how you view your own love stories.

Trust me, there were times along the journey that I was tempted to return to that familiar story of "this will never work out—they aren't the one" or to notice my partner's behavior as evidence that the relationship was doomed, but that would have been missing the point almost entirely.

When I surrendered to the truth that everything I saw in my love was Life showing me something I needed to see in myself, everything changed.

The relationship became a catalyst for growth, and a healing gift, to help me see all the untrue stories I was believing that kept me (or pulled me) out of my Higher Nature, the place where miracles happen and we witness a beauty so profound that it can accurately be described as holy.

This insight helped me understand the difference between experiencing ourselves (and others) as broken and imperfect, instead of the truth that we are whole and complete—perfect as we are AND we just happen to yet believe a few things about ourselves that aren't true. These stories are what keep us in our shadow, our Lower Nature.

Everything in life is trying to show us who we are. And when we surrender, we behold the miracle.

When I embraced this final lesson that not only were the negative emotions projections, but also the love I was feeling for my lover was actually for—and within—myself, then I fully surrendered to Life and its gentle, loving whisper.

I finally saw that Life was always pointing me back to myself in order to see who I truly was from the beginning: Love.

That's what Life does for us all. It sees us as whole, and everything it gives us in the beautiful, messy ride is just designed to show us that truth.

And so, "let's stay here" is an invitation to be present, to breathe deeply and embrace the richest human experience possible: love.

Whether it's in a relationship, our career pursuits, social interactions, our lens of the world around us, or in making the most of the moment right in front of us, it's a call to surrender our fears, our worries, our basest instincts—our lower nature, the part that sees the need to protect ourselves (from things that won't literally kill us)—and to embrace our highest selves. To operate from a space of love, not fear; of expansion, not contraction; of light, not dark. To dwell in that space of connection to all that lives and is good and noble, not under the illusion of separateness.

It's a call, in every moment, to listen to the still small voice that comes when we open our hearts and cut out all the noise—and courageously follow wherever it will take us.

It's a call to surrender wholeheartedly to the loving arms of Life. It's a call to choose Love.

Let's stay here.

Let's Stay Here

Did you enjoy *Let's Stay Here?*

As an independent publisher, I rely strictly on word-of-mouth support and individual purchases from generous, beautiful people like you. Every book sold counts, and helps me provide for my family.

Thank you, genuinely, for your support.

If you enjoyed Let's Stay Here, the most valuable token of appreciation would be to share a review on Amazon. The more 5-star reviews it receives, the more visible it will become to others who are searching and will help reach those who would benefit from the message of *Let's Stay Here*.

Your honest and generous review would mean the world to me.

To leave a review, visit:
lovetruthpoetry.com/amazon

Ready to live in your Higher Nature?

The poems in *Let's Stay Here* are rooted in a timeless spiritual truth that has been echoed in spiritual and psychological teachings throughout history, but never presented in a simple and obvious manner. This is the concept of your Higher & Lower Nature.

Understanding the distinction between your higher and lower natures is essential to living a peaceful, fulfilling life. It can mean the difference between . . .

- living in peace, or feeling disconnected from yourself

- being open to love, or closed off

- seeing clearly, or being led astray by projections

- feeling supported by a loving universe, or remaining a victim of circumstance

In which state would you rather live?

As a special gift to readers, I've created a free cheat-sheet to help you recognize when you are in your higher nature or slipping into your lower nature. With this resource, you can learn how to consistently rise into your higher nature and live the love-filled life you deserve.

Get your copy of the Higher Nature cheat-sheet for free at lovetruthpoetry.com/highernature

Are you ready to find the love you deserve, or are yearning for?

Tired of feeling heartbroken?

Ready to invite more love into your life?

Whether you're trying to heal a broken heart, attract a new partner, or strengthen your current relationship, I've prepared a special gift to help you achieve the love and intimacy you desire.

Get started by downloading our free Love Heals guide, which provides a step-by-step process to help you identify and overcome the barriers in your love life. Learn how to heal old wounds, open yourself up to love, and create the fulfilling relationships you deserve.

Ready to transform your love life?
Download the Love Heals guide today at lovetruthpoetry.com/loveheals

Made in United States
Troutdale, OR
07/26/2023

11565534R10100